The Corporate Sales Formula

The 4 Steps to Turn B2B Prospects Into Clients

By Yaron Sinai

www.corporatesalesformula.com

The Corporate Sales Formula
The 4 Steps to Turn B2B Prospects Into Clients
Copyright © 2015 by Yaron Sinai.

ISBN: 978-0-9891559-1-5

Printed in the United States of America

Date: 06/19/2015

Table of Contents

Chapter 1

The Three Sales Cycles of a Business

In this book, I'm going to share with you what that I've learned about business-to-business sales – as well as running a successful company. Along the way, I'm going to provide you with a powerful way of *Formalizing the Sales Process.* This simple, step-by-step tool will give you the edge that you need to succeed. By streamlining your sales process, you will put a transferable, proven system in place that takes the worry, stress and hassle out of sales – and lets you enjoy the success you deserve.

But first, let me tell you how all of this started: I founded Elementool in 2000. Elementool is an internet software company that sells a Software as a Service project management system to companies, mainly in the United States and Europe. Despite its share of obstacles, the company has survived the burst of the dot-com bubble, (which happened the same year I started my business,) the economic crash of 2008, and the statistics that say that 90% of companies don't survive the first five years of operation.

Before starting Elementool, I worked for a software company as a project manager, met people who were also project managers, and, at the time, I quickly realized there was no good and easy solution for running projects.

So I learned programming at home and worked in the evenings and on weekends for six months straight to build the website that would eventually become Elementool.com.

At the beginning, it was a very simple issue-tracking and help desk solution hosted and offered on Elementool's website. The website was offered for free to people who wanted to use it to run projects. Despite being built by a non-programmer, I am proud to say that it was the first web-based software of its kind in the world.

A few months later, I realized that running Elementool required my complete attention, so I quit my day job to run the website full-time. But it wasn't as easy as I thought it would be. I had to move back with my parents because I couldn't pay my rent anymore. I had no job, no car, and, let me tell you, living with my parents was *tough*. I certainly couldn't get any dates with women during this period (which made things even worse).

To take my website to the next level, I tried to raise funds from investors. And, wanting to look professional, I rented a laptop from a nearby computer store every time I went to a meeting with investors, because I didn't have enough money to buy my own laptop computer at the time. Laptop computers used to be expensive in those days.

Each time I stepped out of a meeting, no matter how well or how badly it went, all I cared about was the fact that I had just wasted $40 on the laptop, instead of getting something to eat. After a few meetings like that, I realized that I was wasting my time and money, so I decided to skip seeking investors and try to grow the site on my own.

And grow it did. Soon I hired a group of programmers who developed additional products and added more features to make the system more sophisticated. People were happy with the new web-based solution and the company continued to grow.

Fast forward to today: since Elementool was founded, over 45,000 accounts have been opened. Some of the largest companies in the world, including Best Buy, Burger King, DirecTV, Mitsubishi, AvisBudget, Honda, State Street Bank, GE and many others, depend on Elementool to help them improve their workflow.

But how did it happen? How did I go from renting a $40 laptop for business meetings to growing a world-class company trusted by many of today's Fortune 500 companies?

It wasn't by accident. I used the same determination I had to build the company to grow it as well – through sales. Once my company, my product, my key staff and my delivery systems were in place, it was make or break time. I knew I had created something that could help millions of people, but how did I go about telling them about it?

One thing they don't teach you while building a company is what to do once it is built! Suddenly I had to switch hats from founder, programmer and CEO to salesperson, and it wasn't easy. However, the strategies I used along the way are what constitute the bulk of the book you're reading right now.

The Three Sales Cycles of a Business

Selling is not a destination; it's an evolution. In other words, what works when your company is starting up would not necessarily work once it is up and running, and what works when it is just starting out would not necessarily work when it is mature and, by all accounts, already successful. That's why you need to recognize what I call **The Three Sales Cycles of a Business**:

The First Sales Cycle of a Business: *Awareness*

When you're first starting out, your needs are very different from when your business is growing and/or already grown, or "mature". In the beginning, you need to build awareness about your product, service, company, brand, locations, offerings, etc. This phase is very active, deliberate and sets a far different pace then the other two sales lifecycles.

It is very common that when you offer a new solution, your target audience is unaware of the benefits that your solution offers – at least, in the beginning. They are used to doing things the "old way" and it is your job to increase their awareness and understanding. That means you have to explain to them why they should switch to your product and how they will benefit from it.

Elementool's project management system is offered as what is known as a Software as a Service, or SaaS. Today, cloud solutions for everything from storing work files to personal photos, music and videos are very common and have become a big part of our daily lives. But during the first few years of Elementool, there were hardly any cloud-based services and people weren't sure about the concept. If you wanted to buy software in those days, you had to order it on CD in a box and install it on your computer yourself.

The terms "SaaS" and "Cloud Service" didn't exist back then. There wasn't even a name for this kind of product. Later it was called "ASP," which stands for Application Service Provider, then it was changed to "SaaS" and now, when everyone uses hosted solutions, they are just called "Cloud".

I remember people used to call and ask us how they could install Elementool. Others were worried about hosting their data with us and I used to be asked frequently, "What will happen to our data if Elementool goes out of business?" To solve this problem, we added a feature to Elementool that enables clients to download a self backup of their account anytime they wish.

In other words, we had to educate the market about the importance of using a project management system and also of the benefits when using a SaaS solution instead of installing it on their network. Until they were made aware of its many benefits, customers were uncertain about buying Elementool.

The Second Sales Cycle of a Business: *Capturing*

Once you've created awareness about your product/service and have started to build buzz, then comes the "Golden Age" of sales when clients come to you. Here it is not so much about creating awareness as "capturing" the many leads that come to your door as a result of what you did in the First Sales Cycle step. During this phase, all we really did was advertise online and then clients signed up to the service. The focus was less on sales and more on marketing.

During this critical lifecycle, potential clients start to understand the benefit in using the product or service that you offer and start looking for it. They hear about it from other people and want to join the trend.

Since the market is generally still evolving at this point, you have little competition. This makes it easier for prospects to find you and they have fewer competing products to choose from.

We reached this point after only a few years in business. Social media didn't exist then, so we used to advertise on different websites that were related to software development, and on various search engines, (some of which, such as Altavista, don't even exist anymore.) We also sponsored several forums and email lists about software testing and development. Since there wasn't much competition, it was easy to stand out and get new clients just from advertising alone.

Later on, as competition grew, more companies began to compete with us on the advertising space. Online advertising got very crowded and expensive. The response rate dropped. It became harder to find clients just from advertising and that's when we started direct sales.

The Third Sales Cycle of a Business: *Maturity*

Finally, the *Third Sales Cycle* happens when the industry matures and becomes very competitive. Other companies offer similar products or services to yours. Buyers have many options to choose from - sometimes too many options, making it hard for prospects to choose the right product since most of them seem the same.

So, how *do* customers choose? The easiest way for buyers to differentiate between the many solutions out there is by price. When all products are the same, they often go with the cheapest product. This is when advertising is no longer enough. You need to find something special to offer your prospects and find ways to get clients in other ways, such as direct marketing.

One of my mentors, Dan Kennedy, the author of *No B.S. Direct Marketing* (Entrepreneur Press, 2013) says, "It doesn't matter what business you are in, first and foremost you are in the sales business." I took this advice to heart and, over the past eight years, I've learned everything I could about sales.

I read many sales books, went to sales seminars, hired $3,000 an hour sales coaches, and, most importantly, tried all the methods that I've learned in the field. I studied the behaviors of customers and tracked how users come to us online. I've watched what my closest competitors do, and don't do, and learned from their successes as well as their mistakes. I've listened and participated in numerous sales calls and product demonstrations that my sales team in Elementool had conducted. I've also learned on the street, in my own life, from how I learn to buy products and what companies did to "sell" me on their product, service or brand. (Every day I get a few sales calls at my office and many sales emails from other companies who try to sell me their stuff.)

Ultimately, I found the way that works best for me by collecting the most effective solutions from different sales techniques that I've learned and then putting them to use to streamline my own sales process.

Now it's your turn.

Streamline Your Sales Process

I used to think that selling is a natural born talent. You either have it or you don't. But now I know that selling is a learnable skill. You can learn how to sell, and I'll show you how in this book. Too many people ignore the **Three Sales Cles of a Business** at their own peril. They apply the same sales strategies that worked for one phase to all phases and, along the way, miss the opportunities that are unique to each phase.

Looking back at my career now, I know that it is important to start the sales operations right from the very beginning. Even if you are still in the awareness phase, sales should be a significant part of your budget, efforts and mindset. In fact, you should start planning and strategizing your sales operations even when you are still in the product development stage, even before you have a product.

Everything has to be planned to support your sales. When you develop your product, you should have it in mind that the product design should help sales. The features you develop, the graphic design, the way you present your brand, colors, names, etc., they all should be considered in advance to support sales and make the product easier to sell.

The Takeaway

No one told me any of this when I first started my own company. I had to learn it all by hand, through experience, trial and error, and as it happened. I don't want the same thing to happen to you. That's why I wrote this book.

Now you won't have to make the same mistakes I did, because on the following pages I'm going to tell you exactly how to avoid them. So, if you're ready to learn more about **The Three Sales Cycles of a Business** and *Master the Corporate Sales Formula*, your journey awaits on the very next page.

Chapter 2

B2B Versus B2C Selling

All selling might seems to be the same, and in many cases the same principles apply across every type of industry, and every size of company. You have to pique a consumer's interest, make them aware of your product, educate them about its features and benefits, impress them with your unique brand, and then "close" them on the deal at hand.

However, there is a fundamental difference between selling to businesses – entities with many potential "gatekeepers," decision makers, and purchasing policies in place – and individual consumers. In particular, the decision making process tends to be different between selling from a business to another business, known as B2B selling, and a business selling to a consumer, known as B2C selling.

Whether we realize it or not, we are all exposed to B2C selling in our daily lives. There are advertisements everywhere we go: on the subway, TV, radio, in our magazines, and in newspapers, be it in print or online.

We buy something at a store and they want our email addresses so they can get in touch with us. What for? They send us coupons, mostly, but just as frequently they send ads to lure us back into their store or to shop online. People try to sell us perfume and sunglasses and jewelry polish every time we go to the mall or a department store. Everyone, it seems, is trying to sell something to someone.

Because this is the sales method that we are most familiar with in our daily lives, it is only natural for us to want to use the traditional B2C approach when we sell our own products to other companies in a business-to-business setting. But selling the B2C way instead of the B2B way can actually hurt you by causing the opposite effect and, in the process, drive away potential clients.

That is why it is fundamental to understand the difference between business-to-business selling and business-to-consumer selling. This chapter will look at the major differences between B2B and B2C selling, then instruct you on the B2B process so you can use it more effectively.

How Consumers Buy: *Decision Making for Individuals*

When it comes to selling to a consumer, the decision making process becomes streamlined because there is typically only one person – or in some cases a very few people – that make the buying decision. In most cases, the individual consumer ultimately makes the decision if she wants to buy.

She knows her budget, knows what she needs, knows what features and benefits are attractive to her, and, in general, decides fairly quickly whether or not to buy. This significantly shortens the sales process, which can usually be completed in one simple transaction because the sale typically only affects the individual making the purchase.

This is true both online and in brick and mortar retail stores, where the decision making process is often the same for, say, buying a book, purse, or movie online and picking up some laundry detergent, trash bags or milk at the grocery store.

The consumer buying process generally looks a lot like this:

- **There is a need for something.** Let's say, in this case, the laundry detergent is running low. (But it could be anything, from buying software or insurance online to purchasing running shoes or a skirt in the store.)

- **The need grows more urgent.** The detergent is almost out and the consumer knows there will be a lot of laundry to do over the weekend. She needs detergent now!

- **The consumer shops to fill that need.** She goes to the local grocery store to buy detergent.

- **The consumer is presented with a variety of options.** There are a variety of detergents to choose from, ranging from the low end of the spectrum – including the store brand and several "off" brands she's never heard of – to the higher end, where she recognizes name brands in lots of different varieties, such as lilac smelling, no scent, allergy free, etc.

- **The consumer goes through an internal process to narrow her choices.** This might include reading some information, be it on the package or online, plus weighing several other options such as price, packaging, size of product, etc. She may be in a hurry and not want to buy in bulk, she may not have been happy with the detergent she chose last time, they might be out of her favorite brand, etc.

- **The consumer makes a choice.** Generally the consumer will narrow the field down to two or three choices, then narrow them down further to ultimately arrive at the detergent she knows she is going to buy that day.

- **The consumer buys.** She makes the purchase, has her needs filled, and won't need detergent for another few weeks. Problem solved!

Now, this process might take a bit longer – and involve more decision makers – to close a sale in case of a large transaction such as buying a car or a house. In these cases there might be other people involved in making the decision, such as a spouse or significant other who will want to weigh in on the purchasing decision as well.

Other people may be involved in the collateral sense: parents who might advise you in their experienced view, friends who've just gone through the process to help you walk through it, etc. Regardless, the decision to buy – even with a big ticket item like a car or house – will ultimately be up to one or two individual consumers.

Often consumer sale price on individual items is low. That means that the risk for the buyer is low as well. In the case of our consumer who needed detergent, her decision making process was aided by fact that it was low impact, low risk, and low cost. If she bought a detergent for five or six dollars and she didn't like it, okay, she lost a few dollars. It might be upsetting, but there will be no long-term financial damage as a result of this transaction.

It also won't affect anyone else. Sure, the clothes might not smell as fresh or feel so soft, but once the "bad" detergent runs out, she can make a better buying decision next time and no harm, no foul. So when consumers make a buying decision on their own and the purchase turns out to be wrong and no one else knows about it, they would not face any embarrassment from making a bad purchase.

A consumer sale is often a short term, one time sale. A consumer buys a product, for example a TV, and that's it. They walk in the store, consider a few choices, maybe talk to a salesperson, make a decision, make a purchase, take the TV home, and they're done.

If the sales experience was good, they might return to the store where they bought the TV to purchase another product in the future. If not, there are plenty of other places selling TVs out there nowadays, and they'll take their business elsewhere. This is the freedom of consumer shopping – no strings, no loyalties, no commitments, no muss, no fuss.

Finally, individual consumers make individual choices. In other words, when consumers experience a problem that they need to solve by buying something – for example, they are hungry, their car broke down, they need insurance – they experience the problem firsthand.

They have a physical or emotional connection to the problem. That makes it pressing for them to solve it. Also, the problem remains their own and goes with them whenever they go. The problem still exists when they go home from work, when they watch TV at night, and when they wake up in the morning, creating a sense of urgency unique to individual consumers.

How Companies Buy: *Decision Making for Corporations*

Now that we've just seen how individual consumers make buying decisions, let's see how companies do it. For one thing, the problem that corporate employees/buyers face – and that needs to be solved now or in the future – is not theirs alone.

The problem is, in fact, the company's problem, not their own personal problem. When they go home at the end of the day, they leave those problems aside until the next day. They might even forget about them once they leave the office for the day. At least, until the next day when they are back at work and the problems become "real" for them again.

When they switch jobs to a different company, they leave the problems behind to get new problems in their new workplace. Therefore, the need to solve a corporate problem is not as burning as the need a consumer has to solve an individual problem like buying milk for the family on the way home.

There is also a large budget difference between consumer and corporate clients. An individual consumer's budget is limited to their salary or savings account. As a rule, this generally means that their spending volume will be smaller. Also, they spend their own hard earned money so they make choices differently, as opposed to a B2B client who essentially spends "other people's money".

As a result, making a mistake and spending money on a product or service that turns out to be unsuitable isn't taken personally by the individual B2B clients. After all, the company lost the money and not them personally. I bet you have encountered more than one situation in which companies spent a lot of money on "white elephants," i.e. projects that eventually got shut down and all the money that has been spent on them was lost.

Companies naturally have larger budgets at their disposal, giving B2B clients more spending power. Therefore, sales to corporations can be much larger, as a rule, than to individual consumers. This makes them bigger not just in price but, in many cases – as we will shortly see – more complex when making the sale as well.

Most large corporate sales involve long-term relationships between the seller and the buyer. For instance, buying software from Company A may involve post-sales training on how to use the software, ongoing support and maintenance for items like upgrades or software patches or even re-purchasing the same service or product in the future.

The B2B Sales Process

Not only is the seller dynamic different in B2B sales, but the buyer's dynamic is as well. In the case of business sales, for instance, it is very likely that there will be a few key people involved in making a decision about the purchase.

In small trades, it might be one person who has a certain budget to spend without approval. But as the purchase price grows, more people need to get involved and approve the sale. It only gets more complicated the bigger the company is, and you can only imagine how complicated the B2B purchasing process is at a large, household name, Fortune 500 company.

Typically speaking, in any B2B sales the individual in the corporation making the actual purchase needs to get their upper management approval, needs to secure the budget *and* get approval of the finance department. The sale often affects more than just the individual who is your contact person in the company. It can affect an entire team of people, a full department and sometimes the entire company. In these cases several people have a say in the decision making process, and they might have different opinions about the product or service being considered.

Anyone who's ever worked in a company, particularly a large company with sizable teams, departments and divisions knows the politics that often go into making a simple choice. When it is difficult for five or six people to agree on where to go to lunch on Friday, imagine the internal decision making process over spending tens of thousands of dollars on a new cloud-based system!

This puts the point person for the sale in an awkward, even unstable position. If they make a key buying decision and, after buying the product, it doesn't quite meet the department's expectations, they can risk their reputation in the company and might even lose their job. Therefore, they need to be very careful before committing to a new product or service, especially if the product's cost is high.

Unlike the more immediate, even instant decision making process when a consumer buys something – in a store or online – the length of a B2B sale can take weeks, and even months. It requires several calls and meetings, then more calls and meetings, then more meetings that are often rescheduled over and over again.

After all that, the ultimate buying decision might take weeks to complete. Sometimes a company's needs change during the actual sales cycle, particularly if it goes on for an extended period, and you will need to adjust or change your offer completely to satisfy the company's new direction.

Elementool and the Sales Process

In my experience, when we sell Elementool's software to new clients, it takes weeks to close a deal. That's not uncommon at all. After all, the prospects are busy people and have many things on their plate to take care of as part of their job. For instance:

- Meetings get rescheduled, pushed from this week to the next week, and beyond.

- Conference calls get dropped at the last minute because one of the principles gets sick, or another conference goes long, etc.

- Someone loses the .pdf files you sent over containing the product qualities they asked for, so they need to be resent.

- After a product demonstration, the client may want to "think about it," check other options, see what else is out there.

- After a demonstration one week, they might call back the next week, wanting to get the whole team on board and have another demonstration with *other* department heads.

- They need to get the budget nailed down.

- Sometimes the legal department needs to review the service agreement (this in itself can take weeks).

- And so on…

Here at Elementool, we've had cases in which the clients were ready to close the deal and start using the service immediately, but had to wait a few weeks for the legal department to approve the agreement.

During that time we were worried that something might happen in the meantime and the sale would be canceled. But if you are flexible and willing to accept the proposed agreement changes, then most likely these kinds of delays will not cause you to lose the sale.

Avoid the Museum Tour: *Putting Benefits Over Features in Your Sales Presentation*

For as long as things have been being sold, selling to consumers has traditionally been based mostly on presenting the product's features. For instance:

- **The car gets 42 MPG**
- **The camera has a 25x zoom**
- **The flashlight is waterproof**
- **The MP3 player holds 100,000 songs**
- **The apartment has 3 bedroom and 2 bathrooms**

When selling to companies, the natural approach would be to sell the product's features as well, right? After all, this is what we are used to when someone tries to sell *us* something. From participating in numerous product demonstrations when we presented Elementool to potential clients, I actually found that corporate buyers *do* expect to be presented with features when they look into a product.

We call it the "museum tour". A "museum tour" is an overview of the product's list of features from start to end. Sounds like it would be beneficial for the consumer but, in fact, the "museum tour" is widely known as the product sales killer. It will cause prospects to get bored and lose interest in the sales meeting within fifteen minutes.

One of the biggest mistakes that sellers make when they sell a product in the B2B environment is to do the feature-focused presentation, i.e. the museum tour. So, what should they be doing instead? When selling B2B, your primary focus should be on the benefits that your product offers to the clients and the problems that it solves them. The secondary focus should be on the features. The features are the means to getting the benefits and solving the problems.

For instance, let's re-examine our original list of "features" and lead with benefits and problem solving first:

- Save gas, money and time with our new car, which gets 42 MPG.

- Take professional quality photos for a fraction of the price with our new affordable camera, which has a 25x zoom.

- Go anywhere, even diving, with our new flashlight, which is waterproof.

- Take a record store's worth of your favorite songs in your pocket with our new MP3 player that holds 100,000 songs.

- Have room for your library, your den, your entertainment center, your art studio, or your guests in our newly listed apartment, which features 3 bedroom and 2 bathrooms.

See how the benefits begin to personalize the features? They answer the "what's in it for me?" question most individual consumers ask when reading a list of features. It might sound counter-intuitive and confusing, and it's a challenge for most companies. But don't worry; I'll talk about it in greater length in the next chapter.

Pushing the B2B Deal Through

So, where does all this leave you? Well, it is your job to push the sales though the corporate channels, whatever they may be, however many "layers" of stakeholders you have to pass through to get the decision made, as long as it takes.

Being proactive will help avoid some of the usual delays and help speed the process along, if not exactly making it "speedy". For instance, don't just sit and wait for the legal department to finish the agreement review. They have many other, more pressing contracts to handle first and if you just let it wait, it will get pushed down the priority list.

How can you go about this most effectively? Be direct. For instance, if a deal needs to be approved by another department, such as finance or legal, I prefer to get the contact details of the people in the finance or legal department and follow up with them directly, instead of waiting for the prospect to follow up.

Given the fact that the prospects themselves are busy with so many things, it is possible that they will not have time to follow up with the other department. If you leave the follow up process to them, it can take months for the deal to be closed. It is your responsibility to make sure that the deal flows through the corporate channels all the way to getting approved.

Summing it Up: *The Major Differences Between B2C Selling and B2B Selling*

Clearly corporate, or B2B clients are different from consumer, or B2C clients, on a variety of levels. Let's look at a few of them more closely now:

- **Fewer people involved:** The amount of people involved in a B2C versus a B2B sale can differ greatly…

- ○ **B2C:** Consumers typically make purchases individually, except in the case of bigger ticket items which may require consulting with one or more people.

- ○ **B2B:** Corporate sales may require approval from entire teams, divisions, and departments before going through.

- **Personal problems:** The amount of problems, or "pain," produced during a B2C versus a B2B purchase varies greatly...

  - ○ **B2C:** If an individual consumer makes a purchase, the problems are personal because it is happening to an individual.

  - ○ **B2B:** In a company, the individual making the purchase is doing it on the company's behalf, making it far less personal than a B2C purchase.

- **Time to buy:** There are huge differences in time to buy...

- o **B2C:** Individual consumers can make decisions almost instantly, in person or online, making their purchases faster and more streamlined.

- o **B2B:** Because of the amount of people, politics, and paperwork typically involved in a corporate sale, B2B sales generally take far longer.

- **Budget size:** Budgets can vary widely as well...

  - o **B2C:** The average consumer makes small-budget decisions on a daily basis, with most purchases smaller than $100 or less.

  - o **B2B:** The size of B2B budgets can range from the thousands to tens of thousands to millions, making the decision making process far more complex.

- **Risk versus reward:** Finally, let us examine the different risks versus rewards in the consumer versus corporate world...

  - o **B2C:** If a consumer buys something and doesn't like it, the risks are generally very low because of the equally low cost(s).

o **B2B:** Meanwhile, the B2B buyer may have his or her job at risk if the purchase doesn't meet expectations.

That is why, from your perspective as the seller, it's so important to design the sales process around building a relationship and providing value to the client over the long-term and not about just closing a deal and moving onto the next. (Don't worry, I'll talk more about how to do this later in the book.)

The Takeaway

It's important to know the difference between B2B sales and B2C sales because, while similar, those differences can make or break a big B2B deal. As we've just seen, the personal may be taken out of the B2B buying decision, but the stakes are much higher, thus making the sale larger and more complex.

Understanding that complexity is the first key to mastering B2B sales, which is what this book is all about.

If you approach the B2B sales process the same as a B2C, it might work against you and cause you to lose sales. B2B sales is more about building a relationships and takes longer to close than B2C. If you try to close a deal on the first sales call, it might present you as pushy and "salesy". It might create pressure on the buyer's side, and that will cause them to avoid your calls because they feel like you just want to "close a deal," and they are not ready yet and need more time to evaluate and think about things.

Also, consumer sales is focused more on features and price, whereas corporate sales is based more on relationship and trust. If you only focus on features, you won't build trust with your corporate prospects because they'll feel that you don't understand them and that will cause them to walk away.

As we have seen throughout this chapter, there is a lot that B2C sales can teach us about B2B sales, but only if we recognize why certain efforts in B2C sales are successful and why B2B is so different. Ignoring the differences can cost you clients, time, energy, money and, importantly, sales. If you have been treating your B2B clients like individual consumers, stop, back up, look around, and learn how to treat them like the B2B customers they really are.

This will allow you to focus more on benefits, and less on features, more on relationships and less on closing, more in trust and less on price. You and your customer will both benefit, leading to increased sales now and in the future.

Chapter 3

Know Your Decision Makers

There is a popular saying that states a good sales person can sell "ice to the Eskimos," which essentially means that a good salesperson can sell anything to anybody. I don't necessarily believe that to be true.

It does not matter how good your sales people are and/or how good your sales process is. They will both fail miserably if they're trying to sell your product to the wrong prospects.

It is nice to talk to anyone who is willing to listen to you, because then you feel like you are selling your products. I often get sales calls from companies who try to sell me products or services that are irrelevant to me and I have no need for, and still

I'm impressed by what they have to say and even how they have to say it.

But talking is not selling. The "numbers game" is not how many leads you collect or people you talk to. It is how much money is being deposited into your bank account as a result of your sales efforts.

In fact, your salespeople should not be selling just "anything" to just "anybody". They should even reject leads that will not lead to sales. As a result, they can cut out half the work – and get twice the results – merely by learning to target the "right" somebody, also known as a "qualified lead".

This is a very important point, so I want to make it clear. One of the critical factors to your sales success is contacting the right people. Who are these "right people"? The "right people" have two main characteristics:

1. **They have a need for your product.** They may not recognize it yet, and you may need to help them understand the "need," but, after all, that is where

selling comes in. The goal is to find folks who genuinely need your product so that when you help them discover the need, the product essentially sells itself. That is why targeting qualified leads is so critical to effective selling.

2. **They have the authority to make a purchasing decision.** Even the best salesperson in the world will fail if they sell to someone who is not a true decision maker. Decision makers represent true authority, the kind that can make – or break – deals, and it behooves you to spend the right amount of time locating this person rather than trying to "sell upward".

You will learn more about both of these topics in richer detail soon, because targeting leads that not only need your product but have the authority to buy it is what this chapter is all about.

Targeting the Qualified Lead

This all might sound very trivial so far. I mean, of *course* you should only contact people who have a need for your product. Who else would you try to sell to? But as trivial as it sounds, so many companies waste their marketing funds on targeting people who have no need for their offer(s). I bet you have experienced it yourself many times in the past, getting contacted by people trying to sell you things you clearly do not need. It is an absolute and frustrating, waste of time for both of you.

I understand why it happens, though. When a company offers its product to people, it feels as if they are selling; as if they are using the company's resources to actually get new clients. But if they target people who do not need their products, they will not get new clients and will end up just "spending" money rather than "investing" it in actual sales. In this case, it is simply better not to do any marketing activity. The result will be the same – the company will not gain new clients - but at least they can keep the money that would have been spent on marketing to the wrong people.

But I get it. It is very difficult to just sit there and *not* do anything; to *not* try to sell. You want to be proactive. You want to feel that you are taking action to reach your sales goals. That is a very good approach. After all, you'll never achieve anything without taking action. But you should also take action in a smart way – i.e. work smart, not hard – and not just for the sake of "being busy". Working smart means you should only contact people who have a need for a product. If you cannot find them, keep looking. And until you have found them, you should not throw away your marketing budget just to make yourself feel good that you're taking action. Spend your money – and your time – wisely instead by finding the right leads first.

Tips for Targeting Your Sales Leads

So, how to tell if you are targeting someone in need of your product or just spinning your wheels? Here are some simple **Tips for Targeting Your Sales Leads**:

- **Picture the ideal client.** To begin defining who has a need for your product, you should create an image – or avatar – of an ideal client. What do they look, act, sound, and spend like? Picture them, clearly, based on past successes – or a new product or service. You can even give this person a name. Personalizing an ideal client helps make him or her real to you.

- **Mine your current database.** If you already have clients, research your current client base and find out who the best clients are. Start with the ones who are most profitable.

- **Check for common characteristics.** Do they share any common characteristics? The easiest characteristics to start with are general demographics, such as age, gender, education level, etc.

- **Drill down deeper.** Finally, get more detailed about places where they live, company size, industry, job title, and more. Consider the places where your ideal clients like to go to on vacation, the books or magazines they like to read, then drill down deeper to explore their hobbies, physical exercise activity, etc. The more specific you get about your ideal client, the easier they'll be to recognize when you finally find them.

Remember, even though this book is about selling to companies, every sale is about an individual. Think about it: you deal with very specific people within a company. For example, if you offer financial-related software and your ideal clients live in large cities and like to play golf, you may want to look into advertising your product with golf clubs.

The more targeted and specific your market is, the more targeted your efforts should be in reaching your prospects.

I'm not going to discuss lead generation. There are plenty of books about it out there and, frankly, it is beyond the scope of this particular book. However, in the next chapter I *will* show how you can reduce the "phone hand up" ratio by 70% when calling your leads – so stay tuned for that.

At Elementool, we used to advertise on websites that focus on software development, because we target companies who develop software. We used to get many leads as a result of these campaigns, but most of the leads did not generate any sales. We wondered why.

Then we created the ideal client avatar, and suddenly we realized that our target audience does not log on to software development websites because they are not developers. They are the development *managers*. This helped us to switch our marketing efforts to totally different channels. As a result, we have been getting less leads. But the leads are more qualified and the closing percentage rate per 1,000 leads is much higher than it was before.

The bottom line is that the quality of your leads will always win out over the sheer quantity of leads. In other words, you should measure how many clients you get for the amount of money you spend on marketing and sales. Your goal should be increasing the number of new prospects for every dollar spent on marketing and sales.

Getting to Know the Decision Maker(s)

Oftentimes, when you talk to a potential client, you can see quite clearly from your own professional perspective that they can use your product or service and that it can benefit them and improve the way they do their work, but they themselves might not be aware of that. After all, if they felt like they had a burning need for your service, they probably would have bought it on their own by now. If the prospects do not even realize that they want your product yet, that is where you come in. In that case, your job will be to help them *discover* that need.

The ultimate "qualified lead" is someone who can actually make a purchasing decision that results in an actual sale for you and your company. For obvious reasons, this lead is known as a "decision maker".

Decision makers are people with authority in the company who can decide whether or not the company will purchase your product or service. It seems straightforward, but sometimes decision makers are not who they seem to be. Sometimes there are covert decision makers who make the decision behind the scenes. I will explain exactly who they are in this chapter as well.

For now, you need to be sure who the decision makers are before you waste a lot of time, energy, and resources selling to folks who cannot actually decide to buy without approval first. It is not always as easy or clear cut as it may seem to find out who they are. When we started our sales in Elementool, for instance, we ran a lead generation campaign that offered free whitepapers about project management to people in the software development industry in exchange for their contact details.

It was a cost-per-lead (CPL) campaign and each contact cost us between $30-50. We called the leads that were generated from the whitepaper campaigns and tried to sell them Elementool's products. We spent a lot of time and effort trying to convince people who were not decision makers to buy our software. The majority of the people who signed up to download our whitepapers were just looking for free information about project management, but they were not executive level and, thus, had no authority to purchase our software. That was a big mistake on our part and a waste of precious time and marketing budget we could have spent elsewhere on prospects who could have bought the product instead.

Tips for Identifying the Company's Decision Makers

Some people have no influence over the closing of the sale, but are hesitant to say so. In fact, they were more than willing to participate in meetings, answer our calls, and have an opinion –

often a strong opinion – about the proceedings. But at the end of the day, they could neither influence nor help us to close the deal, causing frustration and leaving the bargaining table empty-handed.

How can you avoid this trap? Here are a few simple tricks for identifying decision makers:

- **The easier they are to reach, the less influence they have.** Non-decision makers are usually easier to reach than high-level decision makers. And it feels like if you talk to them and start some kind of process with them, it will lead you to close the deal. Wrong!

- **Consider their job title.** Decision makers come with job titles such as Vice President, Chief Technology Officer, etc. They are usually department heads, company managers, and other type of executives. Identifying the decision maker is easier in small companies where there are only a few levels of hierarchy and a short purchasing process. It gets trickier in larger corporations, where there might be several management levels. In large companies, it can also vary from one company to another. A Vice President level in one bank can have more decision power than a Vice President level in a different bank. There is no formula. You will simply need to start calling and find out yourself. But if you start with someone with a title, it will increase your chances of talking to a decision maker.

- **Ask, don't guess.** At Elementool, two of the first things we ask our leads is whether or not they have the authority to make purchase decisions and what the decision process is in their organization. We do this for a couple of reasons. First, we do not want to waste our time guessing and we do not want to waste their time. We are clear and quick here. If the person is not in a purchasing position, we ask who is. In cases where they don't want to let us know who their manager is, we end the call quickly – but politely – and go back to market research to find out the company's hierarchy structure. Then we contact the decision maker in that company directly and start the sales process all over again with them instead.

Remember, at the end of the day, the only people who can make a decision are decision makers. Focus only on them, even if they *are* harder to reach. Your time would be better spent making sales calls and trying to find new clients than presenting your product to people who cannot buy it in the first place.

Identifying Covert Decision Makers

Here is where things get a little tricky: businesses are full of what I call "covert" decision makers. That is to say, sometimes the real decision makers are not the ones who you would necessarily think of at first, or even who your point person might be on the sale.

For example, you would think that the decision maker is the head of the department, but that is not always the case. Here's why: the team, not the department head, will be the ones who will actually use your product, day in and day out.

Since the department head values their opinions, she will naturally rely on them for guidance during the life of the transaction – whether you know it or not. It can't be helped, nor should it. You are an external provider and so her loyalty will be not only with the company, but with the team she leads.

So while the head of the department might be the actual decision maker in the technical sense, eventually the team will determine whether or not they like your product and that makes them – not their fearless leader – the true (covert) decision makers.

The covert decision makers can be identified during the sales process. You should be aware of that and try to pick up the clues while talking to them. As I mentioned earlier, the best way to find out is simply to ask.

Beware Low Hanging Fruit: *Decision Makers on High*

In addition to navigating covert decision makers, there is also the conflict of how high you need to go on the command chain to reach the true decision maker(s). I will say this much based on experience: it is always better to start your way up and go down (top down) than to start your way down and try to go up (bottom up).

Then again, sometimes you might aim *too* high. For example, Elementool is used by teams and middle management level employees. If we approached a Fortune 500's Chief Technical Officer, who runs the entire IT operations of the corporation, it might be too high a reach.

Why? Because this person usually makes more strategic, high-level decisions about the entire corporation's IT strategy and does not necessarily handle what type of project management system a specific department needs. So in this case, were we to start the sales process and try to get an interest for our product, we would generally approach a lower level executive instead.

While it may sound like a setback, the opposite is true. Here's why: in many cases, when we made initial contact with an executive who was too high for this kind of decision, they would direct us to one of their subordinates, such as a department manager. Now, rather than a cold call, you've got an "in".

So now when you call the department manager and tell them that the CTO has referred you to them, it gives you leverage because then they will listen to you and give you proper attention due to of the referral. So here is a case where starting at the top helped us get to the real decision maker somewhere squarely in "the middle".

On the other hand, starting low and trying to climb your way up does not work as well. Here is why: let's say you get in touch with a low level contact who has no decision power whatsoever; none. Now let's say you wow them with a presentation and are able to make them love your product.

Great! You're in, right? Well, not quite. Now your contact within the company needs to approach their boss to push your product through the purchasing process and get final approval for the buy.

Well, can't we just leapfrog over their head and go straight to the source ourselves? Not always. Usually, in fact, the contact will not agree to disclose their boss' name because they don't want to risk their reputation with their boss in case you call her as a referral from them and their boss does not like you. So they will try to present your product to their boss instead.

That is a great way to get your foot in the door, right? Well, yes and no. The problem is that no one will do as good of a job selling your product as you will. By the time the prospect reaches her boss, she has already forgotten half of what you told her about your product. Nor will she be as enthusiastic about it as you are.

What's more, if her boss is interested and has pertinent questions about how your product works, this person won't be able to answer her manager's questions about your product as well as you because she is simply not informed enough. Therefore, the chances of getting a sale from starting down and climbing up are much lower that starting up and climbing down.

Chapter 4

What is Direct Sales?

According to Wikipedia.org, "Direct selling is the marketing and selling of products directly to consumers away from a fixed retail location." Once upon a time, direct sales involved going door-to-door, or even "store-to-store," on foot and in person, to make a sale face-to-face. Today, of course, modern methods of communication make B2B direct sales much simpler, but far from easy.

What is unique about B2B direct sales is that it gives you the opportunity to reach out "directly" to your sales prospects, or leads. "Leads," as we have discussed, are people who have the potential to become your clients. As we saw in the last chapter, direct selling becomes much easier when you have done the groundwork to find and target quality leads.

There are a variety of different ways to get sales leads. I am not going to go into great detail about lead generation methods. There are many books out there about this subject already, and I urge you to read them if you want to learn more about this fascinating topic. For now, I am just going to discuss the three main types of sales leads.

Word of Mouth

Word of Mouth, or WOM, is one of the most authentic and organic ways of generating targeted sales leads. WOM direct sales relies on three critical factors:

1.) People who are actively looking for the kind of service that you offer and…

2.) Have heard about you from someone and…

3.) Approach you to find out if you fit their needs.

At Elementool – and I am sure most other businesses would agree – this is the type of lead that we like the most because they have a high sales closing ratio. We categorize them as "warm leads" because they come with a built-in level of awareness. In other words, they have already come to the conclusion that they need a solution to a business situation in their company and we do not need to help them discover the hidden problem as we do with "cold leads".

And since they heard about us from someone who is already an Elementool client or used to be one, we start with a high level of trust with them right off the bat. What is more, since they know the person who referred them to us has had a positive experience with Elementool's products, it is more likely that they will have a positive experience as well.

They are motivated because they already recognize internally in their company that they have a problem that needs to be solved and are actively looking for a solution.

Word of mouth leads do not need a lot of trust building on your part; they have already done that by the time they get in touch with you. They are more interested in getting right to the point and talking about how your product can help them. In fact, they might even become impatient if you spend your time trying to build trust instead of talking about how your product can help them solve their problem(s). They will feel like you're wasting their time instead of being a solution provider.

So, where do you begin? The way to handle word of mouth leads is to start the interaction by asking them to share with you the main problems they face and are looking to solve. Be specific. Ask them what they expect from you, and what your service should do for them.

When presenting your service or product, focus only on the parts that are relevant to your prospect. Show them how your product solves the specific problems that they have. Ask for their feedback in real time to determine if they are satisfied with what you've shown them and whether or not they feel that this is the right solution for them. If they are still not sure, dig deeper to find out what is still missing from your solution and expand the presentation of the product to solve the missing issues.

The main disadvantage of WOM is that you have almost no control over who spreads the word about your products. Furthermore, it is a slow process that takes time to build. However, when "warm leads" do result from word of mouth marketing, the direct sales process can flow smoother because the trust building has already been done for you.

Marketing and Advertising

Do not discount the traditional methods of marketing and advertising when it comes to direct sales. Using advertising on different media channels, such as social media and other marketing campaigns, can generate a large amount of leads. The problem then becomes are these quantity leads, or quality leads?

The qualification of the people who have shown interest in your products as a result of marketing campaigns can vary significantly. After years of engaging in such advertising methods, my experience has shown me that you can get people who have no interest or need of your products and just found you by accident by clicking on one of your banners, to people who are actively looking for a service like Elementool and happened to see the advertisements at "just the right time". So in order for you to stay effective and avoid spending your time on people who are not going to become clients, these leads require filtering.

The advantage of marketing and advertising is the ability to reach a large number of people and to broadcast your message to a broader audience than WOM advertising. If done correctly, it can increase your sales dramatically. The disadvantage with traditional marketing is that you have little control over who sees your advertisements and contacts you as a response to them.

What kind of leads will you typically get as a result of advertising and marketing? Warm? Hot? You should treat people who contact you as a result of marketing campaigns as cold leads. Cold leads are people who you have not established rapport and trust with. As a result, these prospects should go through the sales process that I am going to show you in the next chapter.

Direct Marketing

As the name suggests, direct marketing is targeting potential clients directly. Instead of taking the more passive approach of word of mouth, where you just count on other people to do the work for you and refer prospects to you, or advertising where you put your message out there hoping that people will respond to it, in direct marketing you choose your target audience – the exact people you wish to approach and then you initiate contact with them.

If you have more word of mouth leads than you can handle, then you are fortunate and you do not need to advertise at all. But in cases where your target audience is very specific and can't be reached through mass media advertising, or in cases in which advertising alone does not provide enough qualified leads to keep your sales department busy, you should run direct marketing campaigns.

It is also a matter of ROI – return on investment. In some cases, direct marketing can have higher ROI than advertising. In this case, you should prefer it over advertising.

The three main channels of direct marketing are email, cold calling by phone, and mail. Yes, good old-fashioned paper and stamp mail. You might think that companies use mostly email marketing these days, but the opposite is actually true. Many companies still use physical mail as their direct marketing channel.

Direct Email Marketing: *The Pros and Cons*

If you choose to participate in direct email marketing, you're in good company.

Now, you may be wondering, "Should I use email for direct marketing or mail?" Email is the easy choice. Just go and buy a list of emails. Craft a message and send it out to tens of thousands, or even hundreds of thousands of names with a single mouse click.

Sounds simple enough, right? Wrong: because it is accessible and low cost, it is also ineffective because by now companies have overused email marketing to the point where it is "white noise" to most consumers. In other words, the majority of email messages that are sent through email marketing are being ignored by the recipients. They are either blocked by spam blockers or being disregarded and deleted by the receivers without ever being read.

Particularly in the B2B realm, promotional emails get lost in the dozens of higher priority, relevant emails an executive receives every day. Since they are being sent unsolicited, they are considered to be an invasion to privacy by their recipients. And since most of us have a negative bias against such emails, the same way we flinch when a telemarketer calls our home at dinnertime or when we see an annoying flyer under our windshield before driving home, they are mistreated and being ignored or deleted.

Now, I am sure that you are different from the average spammer, telemarketer, or intrusive advertiser. You do not want to "bug" people, but you want them to receive your message nonetheless. After all, the products that you offer are very useful.

Your intentions are good and you want to help the people who receive your emails. But since you have not established any prior connection and trust with them, your target audience does not know that. You are a "stranger" and your direct emails are spam; your direct mail pieces are "junk" mail. So by default they treat your emails the same way they treat other emails – a quick click on the delete button, or by clicking on the unsubscribe link at the bottom of the email.

Also, research has shown that for a deal to go through, it takes an average of eight marketing interactions between a buyer and a potential client, none of which you are getting if recipients are basically "trashing" your direct marketing pieces. As I explained earlier in Chapter 2, a corporate sale is not done impulsively. It requires an ongoing interaction between the buyer and seller.

This means that when someone receives an email from a company advertising their product, even if they have an interest in the offer, a minute after they read the email they get distracted at the office by a different email, phone call or someone who comes into the room with a question. As a result, even if it is targeted to them, useful to them and could solve a problem, they totally forget about it.

If you do not believe me, try this little experiment: Try to remember yourself times when you read an email, watched an ad on TV or saw a banner online and told yourself, "Hmm... that sounds interesting, I should check it out" – and, a few seconds later you moved on to do something else and forgot about the offer. Sure, it happens to everyone, but we want to prevent it from happening to you when you offer your services.

The Art of Cold Calling

Let's talk about cold calling. First, what is it? Cold calling is when you call a potential client on the phone to try and start a conversation about your product. These are not "warm" leads. The people who receive your call won't be expecting it, and have no idea who you are, unless you work for a well-known company.

Therefore, the trust and rapport level starts at zero. People can get nasty when you cold call them. I can understand why. I receive a few cold calls each day from people trying to sell me something. In many cases their offer is irrelevant to me. Not only are they trying to sell me something I do not need, but they do it in a pushy way. It feels like they do not know anything about me, and they do not care whether I need their product or not.

For them, apparently, I am just another name on the endless list of contacts that they need to call on a particular day. Sometimes I even get a recorded message calling me! It is literally not even a human being on the line, just a computer who makes hundreds of calls each day. These calls usually catch me in the middle of something business-related and interrupt my daily schedule.

On the other hand, if you look at it from a different point of view, that being from the seller's position, cold calling presents a unique and valuable opportunity to pitch your product in the most personal way possible. In fact, I reached the conclusion years ago that if you want to acquire new clients in the corporate world, the way to do that is by talking to your prospects on the phone.

B2B sales relies so heavily on building trust and rapport, and it is very difficult to achieve that through a process that relies solely on advertising and emails. This can be done more effectively with word of mouth leads. After all, if they are already looking to buy your product and only have a few questions for you in order to clarify a few points, then you can simply answer their questions by email.

Then again, I have realized that you can also lose word of mouth prospects if you do not establish human interaction with them. Also, if warm leads are not enough to keep your sales team busy and you need to find additional prospects, then you need to expand your reach to the market by actively contacting new prospects – and this can be done by simply picking up the phone and calling them.

The main challenge with cold leads is the "hang ups". In other words, rather than hear you out, the prospect will simply hang up the phone when you call them. They can even add insult to injury by being rude and saying something nasty *before* hanging up. Again, we've all been there, so who can blame them?

At Elementool we have tried to setup product demonstrations through cold leads in the past. As an experiment, I hired someone to sit in front of the phone all day and make at least one hundred calls per day to different leads that I bought from a company that sells contact lists based on different demographics.

The poor guy called about three thousand people in one month. Do you know how many product demonstrations he was able to schedule through his efforts? Zero.

But do not be worried. I am about to show you a way to reduce your hang ups by 70% and make people answer your calls, talk to you politely and even agree to schedule product demonstrations with you.

Direct Mail Marketing

When it comes to choosing between direct email marketing, cold calling, or direct mail marketing – which we will be talking about in this section – it's best to have a specific purpose in mind for each marketing method.

You would be surprised to find out that the two largest online advertising platforms in the world – Google and Facebook – both use direct mail advertising to recruit new advertisers on their websites.

I have received promotional letters in the mail from these two companies with special offers trying to persuade me to advertise with them. Why do they use direct mail advertising when they can use their online platform to promote themselves?

Well, obviously it is because direct mail advertising works!

For instance, here at Elementool, we use direct mail marketing specifically to "warm up" the cold leads. We send the cold leads our "Lead warm up kit" – more on that in the next section – and this essentially reduces the hang up rate by 70%. It is just amazing how this thing works, which is why I am so eager to share it with you.

When sending out direct mail, we look for people who meet our ideal client profile. There are many ways these days to find people's contact details. The most important details that we are interested in are physical mailing address and phone number.

If we do not have a prospect's phone number, then we cannot follow up with them on the phone and start the conversation. And therefore, the lead is useless for us. Also, if we do not have a physical address, then we cannot send the prospect our "Lead Warm up kit" and the lead will be useless to us as well. That is because if we just call them out of the blue, they will hang up on us. So in this case, the two work hand in hand to build rapport and trust, through the combined efforts of direct mail marketing and cold calling.

Now, let me introduce you to our unique direct mail piece.

The Lead Warm Up Kit

Here at Elementool, we send out something we call the Lead Warm up Kit (LWK) to any kind of lead that we have. That's right, even to word of mouth leads. Remember, even word of mouth leads might be shopping around, checking different products, and contacting your competitors. Do not take them for granted. Instead, you should stand out. That is where the Lead Warm up Kit comes in.

Because it is unique to us, this direct mail package helps to differentiate us from any other competition out there. The LWK creates an effect on the prospect side. It is relevant to their world and provides them with value for free at our expense. What's more, it is personal, not an automated email that is being sent out to thousands of people.

When prospects receive their own LWK, it makes you instantly memorable. It makes them wonder who you are and why are you sending it to them. Or even, "What did I do to deserve this?!" It makes you stand out of the crowd.

From listening to hundreds of sales calls over the years, I discovered that sending out these Lead Warm up Kits really helps us to get into people's hearts. Now, I am not saying that it makes them open their wallet and just buy anything you offer them, but they *are* more willing to listen to you – and that is a great place to start a sales call.

Here is why they are suddenly "warm" rather than cold: You went through all this effort to send them something nice by mail, so now they feel that the least they can do in return is listen to you for a few minutes. It also makes them curious about who you are and why you sent them the LWK in the first place. So now, rather than being defensive about your call, they actually *want* to hear what you have to say.

Of course, they agree to open just a crack in the door for you for a short while. And there is much more for you to do, but at least you get a chance to do it now rather than simply hear prospects hanging up on you all day long!

As a result of pulling back on cold calling complete strangers and using the LWK instead, we were able to schedule many product demonstrations and acquire new clients.

So, what is in the Lead Warm up Kit? I'm glad you asked!

The Three Mail Pieces in the LWK

The Lead Warm up Kit includes three mail pieces that are sent one after the other, one week apart from each other. First, a note about appearances: These direct mailers should look like they were sent by a person and not an automated mail service. Here at Elementool, we always write and address the prospect's mail details by hand. And we always use real stamps, envelopes, and packages. This ensures that, when the prospect receives our mail, it looks like a personal letter sent by a real person, not an automated system just going off some paid database by a marketing firm. As a result, we have found that our direct mail gets opened 90% of the time. What's more, when we talk to prospects on the phone, they actually remember receiving our LWK. How is that for a "warm" lead?

I assume that our recipients receive many letters by mail. Therefore, the mail that you send them should catch the recipient's attention and stand out of the many letters and mail pieces they get every day. Here is where **The Three Mail Pieces in the LWK** comes in:

The First Mail Piece

The first mail piece is designed to create an impact and a strong first impression. It should provide value to the prospect, offered to them by you for free. It should be memorable, so when you call them, they remember receiving it. Physically speaking, the first mail piece should be larger than usual. A fat envelope with a book inside, for instance, or a box with something that is relevant to your prospects and part of their professional world.

It should be accompanied with a sales letter and something we call "social proof". The sales letter should focus on the most common problem people in the prospect's industry face and how your product offers as a solution to the problem. Social proof includes quotes and details about your current clients, such as testimonials, awards and industry recognition to show the prospect that people use your products and rely on you in a proven manner.

The Second Mail Piece

The second mail piece should be smaller. We use a standard letter envelope with a smaller insert inside, such as a coffee coaster, a pen, etc. It should also include a sales letter about a different major challenge that your prospects experience in their professional life and present your product as a solution to this challenge.

The Third Mail Piece

The third mail piece should act as a reminder to your prospect of who you are. Therefore, it does not need to be large, expensive, elaborate, or very involved. For instance, we typically just send out a postcard size sales letter. Remember, you have already made your first impression and impact in the previous two letters, so not much more is required here. Still, by providing a brief reminder with this third mailer, you are making sure that the previous two mailers have more of an impact.

The Art of Following Up: *How to Capitalize on Your Direct Mailers*

Once the mailers are sent out, we usually start calling the prospects between 10 to 14 days from the day of sending the first mail piece. We want to give it enough time to arrive and for the prospect to read it, but not too much time so that they forget its strong first impression. This way when we call, the lead is still warm.

Sometimes the LWK gets lost in the mail, or sent to the wrong address and is not being forwarded to a lead. This will show you the difference between a person who received the LWK and those who have not. People that have not received the LWK will have the same behavior characteristics of a cold call lead. Often they will act suspiciously and not believe you if you tell them that you sent them something by mail. They think you are bluffing.

But not to worry: simply ask them for the correct address and send the LWK again. And this time, advise them to expect it by mail. Then call them two weeks later and I promise you that their response will be quite different!

Chapter 5

Formalizing the Sales Process

Now that you have heard *The Elementool Story*, learned *The Difference Between B2B Versus B2C Selling*, become more knowledgeable about *Determining Your Target Audience,* and learned to *Master the Direct Sales Approach*, it's time for us to move you even closer to closing the deal by *Formalizing the Sales Process.*

Winging It Versus Scripting It

When it comes to formalizing the sales process, there are generally two schools of thought – winging it and scripting it. Specifically, here's what those both look like:

80

1. **Winging it** means improvising and doing something with no preparation. It is a common approach among sales people to just start a sales call and work their way through it, trusting their sales experience and intuition to guide them through the sales process. Sales people who prefer this method like to have the freedom to determine the progress of the sales process based on actual events and responses that they receive from the prospect.

2. **Scripting it** involves the use of various sales scripts, prompts, or messaging to ensure that the sales process is streamlined, simple, and easy to follow for new and experienced sales people alike. While there is naturally some wriggle room during the sales call, the script becomes a "safety net" while following a predetermined process.

So, which sales method is better for you? It's the right question to ask, because both have their advantages and disadvantages and come down to the kind of sales culture you've created at your business.

Some companies might flourish by hiring trusted sales people who can think on their feet and essentially wing it to success. Other organizations might benefit from a more structured approach, where less experienced sales people can follow a script and, as they begin to feel more comfortable, perhaps improvise more often.

"Winging It" Explained

When you "wing it," your sales success becomes more and more dependent on your sales people. If you have talented and experienced sales people, they will be able to leverage their talent and experience to bring you new clients. If you have inexperienced sales people, they will not necessarily be able to bring new business to your company, because they lack the experience required to be spontaneous and follow their instincts while on a sales call.

It is very common to have one or a few sales superstars in your team that are responsible for a large part of your sales. For example, in a team of ten sales people, one employee may generate 40% or more of the sales, while the other nine employees generate the other 60% with their combined efforts.

Clearly, it is an advantage to have such a superstar on your team, especially if all your team members are superstars. But superstars are hard to find and even harder to keep. They are constantly being targeted and even "poached" by other companies who have heard of their sales prowess and often offer them a higher salary, more perks, and even bonuses to come work for them.

In this case, if the superstar leaves your company, your sales drop 40%. That is a big risk to take, and you should avoid being in this situation if at all possible.

When you wing it, you do not have an established, proven sales process that generates consistent results. You cannot trust your sales activity to work every time because every time is different. It is dependent on factors that can change any day, such as the mood of your sales team, their ability to be creative on one day versus non-creative on a different day, the reaction that your team receives from clients, etc.

To prevent that kind of a situation, you should design a sales process that is responsible for generating sales. Your sales system – rather than a single sales superstar – should be the factor to your success. It should allow even sales people with little experience to bring in new business and, on top of that, you can add good sales people to improve the results of the sales system.

This brings us to the process of scripting your approach to avoid expecting your sales people to wing it.

"Scripting It" Explained

Scripting, on the other hand, is planning every step of the sales process so that nothing is ever really left to chance. The script determines what the sales person should do and say in advance. In the ideal sales script, everything is taken into account. For instance, if the prospect says "A," you should say "B." If the prospect says "C," you should say "D," etc. This leaves out any room for changing the sales process by the sales person.

The script is a word by word version of what to say to the prospect, from the introduction to the closing. Sales people sometimes object to using sales scripts because it makes them feel like robots, repeating the same lines over and over again.

Then again, there are different levels of scripting. Some companies require their sales people to stick to the script word for word and do not allow them any freedom to improvise, while other companies use the scripts as a reference point only and allow their sales people to make changes to the process flow as the sales call goes forward.

When we started with our sales team in Elementool, we had no scripts. We created a list of benefits and features for each product and had the sales people just call up prospects and run the sales call as they saw fit. As a result, each sales call was different from the next. It was also different from one sales person to the other. Some sales people are better at improvising and thinking on their feet than others. Those that possess that unique skill set were able to come up with answers to prospect's questions on the fly, without referring to a script. For others who are not quite as good at improvising, there was at least a frame of reference for them to use in the "benefits and features" language.

Other sales people are not as good and sometimes get nervous and lose their focus during the exchange. In these cases, the interaction with the prospect did not generate good results and often we lost the opportunity to sell.

Now we have the entire sales process scripted from the initial call all the way to the product demonstration. The scripts guide our sales people in each stage of the sales process, giving them tools that are based on the accumulative knowledge that we have acquired throughout the years conducting thousands of sales calls.

So, which of the two methods do I prefer? I think that scripting is a much better approach than the wing-it sales process.

That's because scripting offers the following advantages:

Consistency

When all your sales people do and say the same thing, you can expect similar results out of their efforts. This way you can compare the performance of your sales people side by side and achieve measurable results. Because they all say the same text, they should all have the same results. The sale is no longer based on their personal talent and ability to improvise.

Of course, there are differences in performance among sales people even if they all follow the same sales process. Talent naturally comes into play, with some sales people reading the script more effectively, perhaps more positively and even energetically, than others. But if your sales process is good enough, even mediocre or inexperienced sales people will be able to close deals.

Also, if an average sales person brings in ten new clients every month, but a particular sales person can only bring in two new clients every month, you can determine that there is a problem with that employee and take the proper action needed to rectify that.

Constant Improvement

A sales script enables you to constantly improve your sales process. When you use scripts and you do not get the results you were expecting, you can experiment and change part of the script to improve the outcome.

When you experiment with the sales process this way, you can change small parts of it and measure whether or not the change improves the results. If it does, embed it into the process for the long term. If it does not, you should try something else. In this way, you are constantly refining the sales script until it becomes nearly flawless.

Speed of Access

With the right script in place, one that has been proven to be effective, new sales people can start selling fast. At Elementool, new sales people can start calling prospects on their second day on the job. They spend the first day learning and practicing the scripts and, on the second day, they start using the scripts on their sales calls.

Of course, there is still a learning curve and it takes them a few weeks to improve their performance as they talk to more prospects, but they do not need to spend days or weeks memorizing product material, benefits, or features. It also enables you to replace sales people faster and does not require special skills or prior knowledge from new candidates. That makes it easier to find new employees for your sales team, with less down time spent in training along the way.

Naturally, it is up to you to decide how closely you want your sales people to stay aligned with the sales script you provide for them. When we have a new employee joining the sales team, I prefer that they just follow the script word by word for at least a few weeks. This gives them the "comfort zone" they need to work off the script and get familiar with it, while also providing the freedom to interject or speak up if they feel the need to during the call.

When they get more familiar with the prospect's needs and the sales process, they still need to stay close to the script, but they can skip some part of it, or change its structure based on the reaction that they receive from the prospect. For instance, if they feel the prospect's impatience or time sensitivity, they might instinctively skip a feature or benefit or passage he does not seem interested in to get to something that might be more effective.

The 3-Stage Sales Process

In general, even after working as a sales person for Elementool for a few months or longer, the script is the backbone of the sales process. And it *is* a process, with specific steps in place to help move the prospect along toward a closing. Here at Elementool, we divide the sales process into three stages:

1. The initial call
2. The consultation
3. The product demonstration

Here is how each of the three steps of the process might look:

Step 1: *The Initial Call*

This is the first step of the Elemental sales process as well as the first point of contact with your prospect. At this point, you have not established any trust or rapport with your potential client, and that is the goal of this stage: to establish some level of trust and rapport to allow you to take your sales process to the second stage.

Because it is critical to get this stage right, you should write a sales script that the sales team will use for this call. If done correctly, it can allow you to start a sales process that would lead to acquiring a new client at the end. If done incorrectly, the sales process with this prospect will end in less than two minutes with no sales or results whatsoever.

Before tackling this stage, take a moment to put yourself in the prospect's shoes: You are calling the lead in the middle of the day, unexpectedly and without any notice. It is very likely that you will catch your prospect in the middle of another activity, particularly a work-related one. Sometimes the person will not be able to talk to you because she is about to step out of the office for a meeting, she is in the middle of a discussion with other people in the room, etc. If this is the case, be respectful, end the call and call back again on a different day.

In case the lead *can* accept your call, you still have only a few seconds to create a good impression to allow you to start a short conversation.

So, what should you say? Remember, there should be a script for this already in place. Specifically, the first sales script should be short and to the point. You only have about 15 seconds to make a good impression, so the goal of each sentence is to allow you more time to talk with your prospect.

During the call the person on the other line will keep asking themselves, "Why is this person calling me?" And, "What's in it for me?" As a result, your script should handle this kind of prospect mindset with ready-made answers whether or not the prospect asks those questions out loud. In your script, make it clear why your salesperson is calling AND what's in it for the prospect. That way they do not have to keep asking themselves!

You should open the call by introducing yourself and the company you work for. Then you should bring up a common and critical problem that your prospect is likely to have, related to the industry and position of your ideal client. Of course, this means that you should conduct extensive market research prior to starting the sales calls and find out the main challenges that your potential clients face. Then pick the one most common and critical problem. Insert this problem into your script. Describe the problem briefly and tell the prospect how your company, product, or service has already helped other people solve it.

Up until now, you have been the only one talking, but naturally you would like to get the prospect involved in a conversation. Questions help elicit responses, so ask her if she can relate to the problem you just described. If you have done a good job in your marketing research, the prospect *will* be familiar with the critical problem that you mentioned. If so, you will have established some trust and rapport. The prospect feels that you know what they are going through.

Now it is time to move on to the second step:

Step 2: *Consultation*

Now that you've introduced yourself and found no objections yet, you are ready to move into the consultation phase. This simply means that you have moved from establishing rapport to problem solving, or consulting, for the prospect.

To make it official, offer the client a free 15-minute consultation in which you will review their current situation and offer ways to improve the process. You want to make sure to let them know that there is no obligation on their side to buy anything and you just are just offering them a free call.

Before scheduling the consultation, find out what the decision making process is in the prospect's company. Remember, if the person is not a decision maker, you should not spend time talking to them any longer. Find out if they are a decision maker, and if they currently use a product or solution similar to yours.

Again, if they already have something in place, are happy with it, and are not looking to switch, most likely you will not be able to sell them your product, so you might want to end the call without offering a consultation.

However, such decisions should be made based on your availability. If you have free time on your calendar and no other better leads, you might want to take your shot with a non-qualified lead and provide the consultation anyway. But if your schedule is full and there are other folks to call, you want to talk to the people who most likely *will* buy your product. If the person is a qualified lead and a decision maker, then schedule a consultation with them and move the sales process to the next phase.

The consultation has a few purposes:

Builds Trust

One of the biggest reasons for the consultation phase of the sales process is to build trust. That's mainly because we use this part of the sales call to provide free information to the prospect.

By giving away valuable information to the prospect, specifically information that the prospect can use to improve his current business situation, we create trust and intimacy with the person we are talking to. It shows them that you are not just there to take and take, like most vendors, but you are also willing to give without asking for anything in return.

Presents You As An Insider

During the consultation call, you and the prospect will enter into a discussion about the different challenges that people in her industry and position face. You will use language and terminology used by people in the industry. It will make the prospect feel that you are an insider, one of "them". You know what they go through. This is a trust building technique, one that inches you closer to the sale with each link of the "trust chain".

I remember one time participating in a consultation we conducted with a prospect. It was scheduled to take 15 minutes, but instead it took an hour and a half. The prospect just poured his heart out. Finally, someone understood and listened to him! At the end of the call, he said that he felt like he just had a session with a therapist. That is one extreme, but not entirely uncommon, example of the power of building trust with a prospect.

Establishes Your Authority

On the call you talk about problems and challenges that most people have in the specific industry you are in, and you offer the prospect solutions to these challenges based on your own experience and research that you have done. This presents you as a knowledgeable expert, one who has both expertise and authority to solve the prospect's problems.

Now, let me ask you a question: When you have a physical issue, who do you prefer to go to – a primary care provider or an expert in what ails you? I would guess an expert.

The same principle applies here. When people are approached by someone to help them with a business issue, they prefer – and expect – that this someone will be an expert in his field. That's because people want to find the best help that they can get.

Let me ask you another question. When you go to a doctor, which medical advice will you take more seriously: a primary care doctor's advice or an expert's advice? Again, I'm guessing you chose an expert's advice over the general practitioner's.

It's the same in business-to-business sales. When people are offered a business solution, they will take this solution more seriously – and naturally be more committed to it – if the solution comes from an expert rather than someone who doesn't seem as well-versed in their particular needs and/or industry.

Helps You Find Out the Prospect's Hot Buttons

"Hot buttons" are emotionally charged issues and problems that someone has regarding a specific topic. Everyone has them, including prospects. We want to find out what *specific* hot button issues the prospect has in regards to the field and industry your product is part of. As I have mentioned earlier in the book, the goal is to find the prospect's main professional challenges in your product's field and offer a solution to these problems using your product.

You simply cannot sell your product if it does not solve a problem. If everything is wonderful in your prospect's world, why would they possibly want to change it by introducing a new service or product? It is critical to find out what keeps your prospects up at night. What problems stop them from getting their business targets? Increasing their revenue? Streamlining their process? Getting more leads? And so on.

You can ask them and they might tell you, but sometimes they are not even aware of the issues that have hurt their business. In that case, you need to help them discover those issues, as discussed earlier – remember, you are the expert. And you do that in the consultation.

This requires you to be familiar with their industry and the common problems and challenges people in their position face. In the consultation you create a discussion about these problems and dig deeper to see if the prospects experience them. If they do, you can elaborate and go into more details about each one of the issues your prospects face. Write down what they are saying. Along the way, they will provide you with inside information about their work and current situation that you can use later in the sales process.

As you can see, the consultation stage requires you to research the market thoroughly and be prepared. Following this sales process and going through the market research that I described earlier will eventually make you an expert in your field. You cannot appear experienced or speak with authority if you do not at least have a working knowledge of the prospect's industry, even the company where they work. But do not be worried; this is an ongoing process of improvement. You might not get it correctly at the beginning, but over time you will be able to identify the main issues that your target market experiences. For instance, there will generally be eight to ten challenges that will be common in the industry and that your prospects will bring up as you speak. The more you talk to prospects, the more these issues will appear, making you more and more familiar with each one – and how to explain how your company solves it.

This stage should also be scripted, of course. You should write down the questions you are going to ask your prospects and the solutions you are going to offer for each one. You should also try to "catalog" every hot button issue you run across and offer a solution for each one.

During phase one, if we feel that the prospect is cooperative and we identify a need for our products, we offer to schedule the consultation. The problem with scheduling appointments to another time is that often the prospects do not show up to the phone call (also known as a "no show").

Sadly, this is all part of the "game". People's schedules can change between the time you talked to them and the time of the meeting. Prospects get cold and forget why they even agreed to meet up with you in the first place. Get used to it and accept it. There is nothing you can do about it, other than persevere and try once more. In this case, you will need to contact the prospect again and reschedule the call. They might not show up, even to a later call. Do not give up. Keep scheduling again until you get them on the call. This is why it is better to progress through the phases on the first call with the prospect.

Sometimes we talk to people that are very communicative and do not rush us off the phone. In this case we do what we call "sliding". Instead of scheduling the consultation call to a different time, we simply *slide* into the consultation while we are on the initial call.

Go with the flow and do all those things you might do in a second, follow-up consultation phone call. Keep going until the prospect stops you. If they do not stop you, keep going and you might even be able to slide into the product demonstration once you have finished the consultation.

Step 3: *The Product Demonstration*

This is where the actual sales process takes place. If done correctly, Step 3 will get you closer to the sale. As mentioned in previous chapters, corporate sales can be a long, drawn out process. Even if everything went well on the product demonstration call, you might not be able to close the sale on this call and will need to schedule follow up calls for later times.

There could be different reasons why this happens. For instance, the prospect might need to get budget approval or to consult higher-ups and show the product to other people on the team (possibly or even their boss.) Or the prospect might be shopping around and checking out other competitive products while still entertaining your offer. Regardless, you always want to try closing the deal on the phase three call as it will be the culmination of all your earlier efforts.

Now that you've established trust and rapport and you also know the main challenges and hot buttons that your prospect has, you should design the product demonstration around it. Here are some simple tips for doing just that:

Don't Fall Into the "Museum Tour" Trap

As introduced previously, a "museum tour" is when you conduct your product demonstration by presenting the entire system from start to finish and going through all the features, regardless of whether or not they are relevant to the client.

We used to conduct this kind of presentation before we realized that the prospects at the other end of the line lose interest in our demonstration in about the first 10 minutes. At the end of the demonstration, which could go on for an hour or more, they were simply overwhelmed with too much irrelevant information that we had provided them about our service. As a result, these product presentations were time consuming and ineffective.

Now, why do I call it a "trap"? Simple: because the museum tour is a very common product presentation by companies out there. For example, if you ask to sign up for a product demonstration of a random company, it is very likely that they will give you a museum tour of their product. So, because it has become the industry norm, this is what prospects typically expect from you. When they join your presentation, they expect to sit back and watch a 30-60 minute product overview. And when you try to do something different by skipping out on this overview altogether, they often object to your different way of doing things, because they are not used to that.

But you should run the show, not your prospects. It is *your* demonstration and you should decide how it goes, particularly when such standard presentations are ineffective and do not produce results for you. The way to run a proper product demonstration is to focus on the hot button topics and the specific problems that the prospect has shared with you during the consultation and then show your prospect how your product offers a solution for each problem.

Let them see for themselves the benefits that they are getting from your service. Your product features are just the means to get the solution that your prospect needs. As such, they should not be the center of attention.

The idea of the entire sales process, from start to finish, is to solve the prospect's problem; period. We need to give them a good reason to start using our products. It might help you to think about it from their point of view. They need to get funding for the service from the finance department, not to mention the fact that they need to get their team onboard using your new products. They probably need to change internal procedures as a result of adopting your solution. It is a lot of work and change on their end. They need to have a very good reason to do so. The fact that your product has blue buttons and nice screens will not be a good enough reason. If your product can solve a problem that keeps them up at night, now *that* is a good reason – and they will act on it as a result.

Once you have done a few consultations and product demonstrations, you will discover that although your leads come from different companies, they face similar challenges. After awhile, you will be able to identify these challenges and you should create solutions for them using your product. You should script it and have your sales team use these scripts when they identify these issues with their prospects.

In this book I am not going to get into different types of sales techniques. There are many books out there that discuss this topic in great length. If you feel that you need more help with that, I recommend that you read additional books about sales that focus on specific sales techniques. However, I *would* like to share a few important sales techniques that you should be familiar with.

Three Methods for Overcoming Objections

Throughout the process your prospects will raise objections to things you say as you try to persuade them to buy your product. It is only normal and completely natural as part of the sales process, so do not take it personally. People have their own opinions and they also sometimes simply do not need, or want, to buy from you. Even if they need your service, people do not like to feel like they just bought something without giving up some sort of a fight. It is human nature. People like to buy but do not like to be sold. The best way to handle objections is through one – of or, if necessary, all – of the following three steps:

Look for repeat offenders

As you talk to more and more prospects, you will begin to hear many of the same objections as they inevitably start to repeat themselves. Write down the objections that you hear from your prospects. Then, at the end of the call, prepare a script that handles each objection and provides a proper solution to it. So next time a prospect comes up with the same objection, you are ready to answer it and jump the hurdle and move forward with the sales process.

For example: if you offer a cloud-based software and your prospects are worried about security so they do not trust a company to hold their data on the cloud, describe the security measures that your system uses to protect their data.

Solve the objections

Not all objections are invalid. Indeed, some might shine a light on why your previous sales calls might not have been as effective as you may have hoped. Analyze the objections and see if they point to a problem with your offer or product. They might see something that you do not see. Solve this objection by offering a business solution to this problem that is specific, clear and mentioned during the sales call.

When we started, Elementool was one of the first cloud-based project management solutions on the market. The concept of hosting data on another company's website was not familiar to many companies at the time. Frequently we used to get the same objection over and over from prospects saying: "What will happen to our data if your company goes out of business one day?"

This was a valid concern. To solve that, we developed a feature that enables our customers to download a backup of their entire account at any given moment. That was a specific solution that helped overcome the objection and, once we began sharing it front and center, it helped solve not only the client's problem but ruled out that particular objection.

Which brings us to our next point...

Handle objections before they occur

If you encounter an objection that repeats itself frequently, and you were able to find a business solution to the objection, make a note of that and share it with your prospects as part of the sales script. If you handle the objection before it occurs, then after, it will create a smoother sales process.

For example: if we know that people are concerned about their data and as a result we developed a feature that enables them to download a self-backup of their account, we can mention this fact in the sales script as we present the product instead of waiting for the prospects to bring it up.

Smoothing Out the Sales Process

A smooth sales process is one that has more agreement from the prospects than disagreement. If the prospect brings up objection after objection and argues about different topics during the product presentation, it creates a negative environment of resistance and pushes the prospect away from your product and damages the trust and rapport that you established with them earlier, resulting in no sale.

But if the prospect agrees to things you say during the presentation, and you are able to solve their concerns even before they are raised, it creates a positive environment and the prospect feels that you see things the same way. It helps increase the sense of trust and even cooperation between both parties, making the prospect feel better about you while reducing any anxiety that they might have as a result of the sales process.

It's all about momentum. Every time a prospect raises an objection, it breaks the momentum and interrupts the trust building and rapport. But when there are fewer objections and those objections that are raised are handled smoothly, efficiently, and expertly, the momentum remains and trust, rapport and cooperation more often result in a closed sale.

A Few Words About Price

Price is one of the most common objections. If a prospect brings up a price objection, it means that – in her opinion – the value of the product is not high enough to justify its cost.

In this case, you need to do one of the following to overcome this very real objection: increase the perceived value of your product or reduce its cost. The value offer of your service should be much higher than its price. The higher the value compared to its price, the more attractive your product is to consumers.

In cases where your product's price is high, the prospect might need to get funding approval and allocate the budget for it. This is an internal purchase procedure and not an objection. If the value that the prospect gains from your product is high enough, in most cases they would be able to find the funding for it.

Selling to Large Corporations

The dream of everyone who sells products or services to corporations is to land a large sale to a global corporation, to sell your product across the board to an entire Fortune 500 company, and, potentially, to have tens of thousands of the company employees use your product – and, as a result, gain a large amount added to your sales quota and your company's bottom line.

Obviously we all want that obviously, and the logical way to achieve it is to contact the Fortune 500 corporation's top management and persuade them to buy your product and implement it companywide. But unless you work for a large, well-known company with a well-established reputation and very strong business connections in high places, I doubt if this is the proper way for you to go. Instead, if you run a small company or you have new products with little reputation, the best way to start is by getting your foot in the door. Starting small and working your way up and across the corporation is likely to be the most beneficial approach for you in this situation.

I have seen it happen again and again here at Elementool. We manage to close a small deal with a small team that works for a large corporation. It begins with just one small project. They start using our product and soon they expand the usage for another project.

Before you know it, more people on the team also start using Elementool for their own projects. The word spreads and after a while other people from different departments hear about Elementool and start using it for themselves. And, slowly, we are able to spread the usage of our product in that company to other departments. Sometime these departments are even located in different countries.

My point is to keep your expectations realistic and do the work. The sales process works best when you work it, consistently following these three simple steps. When you do, not only will the sales process become more streamlined, but more successful as well!

Chapter 6

The Corporate Sales Formula

So far we've covered a lot of ground. From *The Difference Between B2B Versus B2C Selling* to *Determining Your Target Audience*, from *How to Master the Direct Sales Approach* to *Formalizing the Sales Process*, you've had a first rate education in all things sales.

But I would be remiss if I left you without that one line item that will pull everything you have learned so far together. That would be what I call The Corporate Sales Formula. This formula, if followed, could lead to more sales more often, for more profit – period.

It is simple, it is effective, it is proven, and the more you use it, the easier it will get to replicate it for every new sales person you hire. So, what is it? The Corporate Sales Formula contains the following four steps:

- **Step 1:** *Identify Your Ideal Client*
- **Step 2:** *Target Your Ideal Client Directly*
- **Step 3:** *Warm Up Your Cold Leads*
- **Step 4:** *Conduct the 3-Step Sales Process*

Now that we know *what* the Corporate Sales Formula is, let's dig deeper into each step to make sure we can follow it correctly.

Step 1: *Identify Your Ideal Client*

The formula starts with identifying your ideal client. It is commonplace for sales departments to think that being busy is being productive, but your salespeople should not be selling to just "anybody". Instead, they should be reaching out to your ideal client. These are prospects who not only have a need for your product, but actually have the authority to make a purchasing decision.

No matter how ideal the client may be, even the best salesperson in the world will fail if they sell to someone who is not a true decision maker. Decision makers represent true authority, the kind that can make – or break – deals, and it behooves you to spend the right amount of time locating this person rather than trying to "sell upward".

To begin defining who has a need for your product, you should create an image – or avatar – of an ideal client. What do they look, act, sound, and spend like? Picture them, clearly, based on past successes – or a new product or service. You can even give this person a name. Personalizing an ideal client helps make him or her real to you.

Mine your current database. If you already have clients, research your current client base and find out who the best clients are. Start with the ones who are most profitable. Then check if they share any common characteristics. The easiest characteristics to start with are general demographics, such as age, gender, education level, etc.

Finally, get more detailed about places where they live, company size, industry, job title, and more. Consider the places where your ideal clients like to go to on vacation, the books or magazines they like to read, then drill down deeper to explore their hobbies, physical exercise activity, etc. The more specific you get about your ideal client, the easier they'll be to recognize when you finally find them.

Find the Decision Maker(s)

After identifying your ideal client, you must next determine whether or not they are a decision maker. After all, the ultimate ideal client is someone who can actively make a purchasing decision that results in an actual sale for you and your company. For obvious reasons, this lead is known as a "decision maker".

Decision makers are people with authority in the company who can decide whether or not the company will purchase your product or service. It seems straightforward, but sometimes decision makers are not who they seem to be. Sometimes there are covert decision makers who make the decision behind the scenes. I will explain exactly who they are in this chapter as well.

For now, you need to be sure who the decision makers are before you waste a lot of time, energy and resources selling to folks who cannot actually decide to buy without approval first. It is not always as easy or as clear cut as it may seem to find out who they are, but there are a few simple tricks for identifying decision makers.

For starters, the easier they are to reach, the less influence they have. Non-decision makers are usually easier to reach than high-level decision makers. And it feels like if you talk to them and start some kind of process with them, it will lead you to close the deal. Wrong!

Next, consider their job title. Decision makers come with job titles such as Vice President, Chief Technology Officer, etc.

They are usually department heads, company managers, and other types of executives. Identifying the decision maker is easier in small companies where there are only a few levels of hierarchy and a short purchasing process. It gets trickier in larger corporations, where there might be several management levels. In large companies, it can also vary from one company to another. A Vice President level in one bank can have more decision power than a Vice President level in a different bank. There is no formula. You will simply need to start calling and find out yourself. But if you start with someone with a title, it will increase your chances of talking to a decision maker.

Also, be sure to ask, not guess. At Elementool, two of the first questions we ask our leads is whether or not they have the authority to make purchase decisions and what the decision process is in their organization. We do this for a couple of reasons. First, we do not want to waste our time guessing and we do not want to waste their time. We are clear and quick here. If the person is not in a purchasing position, we ask who is. In cases where they don't want to let us know who their manager is, we end the call quickly – but politely – and go back to market research to find out the company's hierarchy structure. Then we contact the decision maker in that company directly and start the sales process all over again with them instead.

Remember, at the end of the day, the only people who can make a decision are decision makers. Focus only on them, even if they are harder to reach. Your time would be better spent making sales calls and trying to find new clients than presenting your product to people who cannot buy it in the first place.

Step 2: *Target Your Ideal Client Directly*

What is unique about B2B direct sales is that it gives you the opportunity to reach out directly to your ideal clients. Naturally, direct selling becomes much easier when you have already done the groundwork to find and target your ideal clients.

There are a variety of different ways to get sales leads. For instance, Word of Mouth, or WOM, is one of the most authentic and organic ways of targeting your ideal client directly. WOM relies on three critical factors:

1.) People who are actively looking for the kind of service that you offer and...

2.) Have heard about you from someone and...

3.) Approach you to find out if you fit their needs.

Word of mouth leads do not need a lot of trust building on your part; they have already done that by the time they get in touch with you. They are more interested in getting right to the point and talking about how your product can help them.

The best way to handle word of mouth leads is to start the interaction by asking them to share with you the main problems they face and are looking to solve. Be specific. Ask them what they expect from you, and what your service should do for them.

When presenting your service or product, focus only on the parts that are relevant to your prospect. Show them how your product solves the specific problems that they have. Ask for their feedback in real time to determine if they are satisfied with what you have shown them and whether or not they feel that this is the right solution for them. If they are still not sure, dig deeper to find out what is missing from your solution and expend the presentation of the product to solve the missing issues.

When it comes to contacting your ideal clients directly, do not discount the traditional methods of marketing and advertising. Using advertising on different media channels, such as social media and other marketing campaigns, can generate a large amount of leads.

The advantage of marketing and advertising is the ability to reach a large number of people and broadcast your message to a broader audience than WOM advertising. If done correctly, it can increase your sales dramatically. The disadvantage with traditional marketing is that you have little control over who sees your advertisements and contacts you as a response to them.

Direct Marketing

As the name suggests, direct marketing is targeting potential clients directly. Instead of taking the more passive approach of word of mouth, where you just count on other people to do the work for you and refer prospects to you, or advertising where you put your message out there hoping that people will respond to it, in direct marketing you choose your target audience. You decide on the exact people you wish to approach and then you initiate contact with them. The three main channels of direct marketing are email, calling by phone and mail.

Direct Email Marketing

Because it is accessible and low-cost, direct email marketing is also ineffective because by now companies have over used email marketing to the point where it is "white noise" to most consumers. In other words, the majority of email messages that are sent through email marketing are being ignored by the recipients.

They are either blocked by spam blockers or being disregarded and deleted by the receivers without ever being read.

Particularly in the B2B realm, promotional emails get lost in the dozens of higher priority, relevant emails an executive receives every day. Since they are being sent unsolicited, they are considered to be an invasion to privacy by their recipients. And since most of us have a negative bias against such emails – the same way we flinch when a telemarketer calls our home at dinnertime or when we see an annoying flyer under our windshield – they are mistreated and being ignored or deleted.

Also, research has shown that it in order for a sale to happen, takes an average of eight marketing interactions between a buyer and a potential client, none of which you are getting if recipients are basically "trashing" your direct marketing pieces.

Calling On the Phone

For this method of reaching out to clients directly where you call a potential client on the phone to try and start a conversation about your product. These are not "warm" leads. The people who receive your call won't be expecting it, and have no idea who you are, unless you work for a well-known company.

Therefore, the trust and rapport level starts at zero. People can get nasty when you cold call them. I can understand why. I receive a few cold calls each day from people trying to sell me something. In many cases their offer is irrelevant to me. Not only are they trying to sell me something I do not need, but they do it in a pushy way. It feels like they do not know anything about me, and they do not care whether I need their product or not.

For them, apparently, I am just another name on the endless list of contacts that they need to call on a particular day. Sometimes I even get a recorded message calling me! It is literally not even a human being on the line, just a computer who makes hundreds of calls each day. These calls usually catch me in the middle of something business related and interrupt my daily schedule.

On the other hand, if you look at it from a different point of view, that being the seller's position, phone calling presents a unique and valuable opportunity to pitch your product in the most personal way possible. In fact, I reached the conclusion years ago that if you want to acquire new clients in the corporate world, the way to do that is by talking to your prospects on the phone.

B2B sales rely heavily on building trust and rapport, and it is very difficult to achieve that through a process that relies solely on advertising and emails. This can be done more effectively with word of mouth leads. After all, if they are already looking to buy your product and only have a few questions for you in order to clarify a few points, then you can simply answer their questions by email.

Direct Mail Marketing

You would be surprised to find out that the two largest online advertising platforms in the world – Google and Facebook – both use direct mail advertising to recruit new advertisers on their websites.

I have received promotional letters in the mail from these two companies with special offers trying to persuade me to advertise with them. Why do they use direct mail advertising when they can use their online platform to promote themselves?

Well, obviously it is because direct mail advertising works!

Step 3: *Warm Up Your Cold Leads*

To "warm up" cold leads, we send them our Lead Warm-up Kit, which essentially reduces the phone hang up rate by 70%. When sending out direct mail, we look for people who meet our ideal client profile. There are many ways these days to find people's contact details. The most important details that we are interested in are physical mailing address and phone number.

If we do not have a prospect's phone number, then we cannot follow up with them on the phone and start the conversation. Therefore, the lead is useless for us. Also, if we do not have a physical address, then we cannot send the prospect our Lead Warm-up Kit and the lead will be useless to us as well. That is because if we just call them out of the blue, they will hang up on us. So in this case, the two work hand in hand to build rapport and trust, through the combined efforts of direct mail marketing and cold calling.

Because it is unique to us, the Lead Warm-up Kit (or LWK) package helps to differentiate us from any other competition out there. The LWK creates an effect on the prospect side. It is relevant to their world and provides them with value for free at our expense. What more, it is personal, not an automated email that is being sent out to tens of thousands of people.

When prospects receive their own LWK, it makes you instantly memorable. It makes them wonder who you are and why you are sending it to them. Or even, "What did I do to deserve this?!" It makes you stand out of the crowd.

The Lead Warm-up Kit includes three mail pieces that are sent one after the other, one week apart from each other. The first mail piece is designed to create an impact and a strong first impression. It should provide value to the prospect, offered to them by you for free. It should be memorable, so when you call them, they should remember receiving it. Physically speaking, the first mail piece should be larger than usual. A fat envelope with a book inside, for instance, or a box with something that is relevant to your prospects and part of their professional world.

It should be accompanied by a sales letter and something we call "social proof". The sales letter should focus on the most common problem people in the prospect's industry face and present your product offer as a solution to the problem. Social proof includes quotes and details about your current clients, such as testimonials, awards and industry recognition to show the prospect that people use your products and rely on you in a proven manner.

The second mail piece should be smaller. We use a standard letter envelope with a smaller insert inside, such as a coffee coaster, a pen, etc. It should also include a sales letter about a different major challenge that your prospects experience in their professional life and offer your product as a solution to this challenge.

The third mail piece should act as a reminder to your prospect of who you are. Therefore it does not need to be large, expensive, elaborate, or very involved. For instance, we typically just send out a postcard-sized sales letter. Remember, you have already made your first impression and impact in the previous two letters, so not much more is required here. Still, by providing a brief reminder with this third mailer, you are making sure that the previous two mailers have more of an impact.

Step 4: *Conduct the-3 Step Sales Process*

The next step of the Corporate Sales Process is to actually divide the sales process into three stages.

Stage 1: *The Initial Call*

This is the first stage of the Elemental sales process as well as the first point of contact with your prospect. At this point, you have not established any trust or rapport with your potential client, and that is the goal of this stage: to establish some level of trust and rapport to allow you to take your sales process to the second stage.

Because it is critical to get this stage right, you should write a sales script that the sales team can use for this call. If done correctly, it can allow you to start a sales process that will lead to acquiring a new client at the end. If done incorrectly, the sales process with this prospect will end in less than two minutes with no sales or results whatsoever.

Specifically, the first sales script should be short and to the point. You only have about 15 seconds to make a good impression, so the goal of each sentence is to allow you more time to talk with your prospect.

During the call the person on the other line will keep asking themselves, "Why is this person calling me?" And, "What's in it for me?" As a result, your script should handle this kind of prospect mindset with ready-made answers, whether or not the prospect asks those questions out loud. In your script, make it clear why your salesperson is calling AND what's in it for the prospect. That way they do not have to keep asking themselves!

You should open the call by introducing yourself and the company you work for. Then you should bring up a common and critical problem that your prospect is likely to have, related to the industry and position of your ideal client. Of course, this means that you should conduct extensive market research prior to starting the sales calls and find out the main challenges that your potential clients face. Then pick the one most common and critical problem. Insert this problem into your script. Describe the problem briefly and tell the prospect how your company, product or service has already helped other people solve it.

Up until now, you have been the only one talking, but naturally you would like to get the prospect involved in a conversation. Questions help elicit responses, so ask her if she can relate to the problem you just described. If you have done a good job in your marketing research, the prospect *will* be familiar with the critical problem that you mentioned. If so, you will have established some trust and rapport. The prospect feels that you know what they are going through.

Now it is time to move on to the second step.

Stage 2: *Consultation*

Now that you've introduced yourself and found no objections yet, you are ready to move into the consultation phase. This simply means that you have moved from establishing rapport to problem solving, or consulting, for the prospect.

To make it official, offer the client a free 15-minute consultation in which you will review their current situation and offer ways to improve the process. You want to make sure to let them know that there is no obligation on their side to buy anything and that you are just offering them a free call.

Before scheduling the consultation, find out what the decision making process is in the prospect's company. Remember, if the person is not a decision maker, you should not spend time talking to them any longer. Find out if they are a decision maker, and if they currently use a product or solution similar to yours.

Again, if they already have something in place, are happy with it, and are not looking to switch, most likely you will not be able to sell them your product, so you might want to end the call without offering a consultation.

However, such decisions should be made based on your availability. If you have free time on your calendar and no other better leads, you might want to take your shot with a non-qualified lead and provide the consultation anyway. But if your schedule is full and there are other folks to call, you want to talk to the people who most likely *will* buy your product. If the person is a qualified lead and a decision maker, then schedule a consultation with them and move the sales process to the next phase.

Stage 3: *The Product Demonstration*

This is where the actual sales process takes place. If done correctly, Step 3 will get you closer to the sale. As mentioned in previous chapters, corporate sales can be a long, drawn out process. Even if everything went well on the product demonstration call, you might not be able to close the sale on this call and will need to schedule follow up calls for later times.

There could be different reasons why this happens. For instance, the prospect might need to get budget approval, or needs to consult higher-ups. They might need to show the product to other people on the team or even their boss, or the prospect might be shopping around and checking out other competitive products while still entertaining your offer. Regardless, you always want to try closing the deal on the phase three call as it will be the culmination of all your earlier efforts.

Now that you've established trust and rapport and you also know the main challenges and hot buttons that your prospect has, you should design the product demonstration around it.

The idea of the entire sales process, from start to finish, is to solve the prospect's problem; period. We need to give them a good reason to start using our products. It might help you to think about it from their point of view: they need to get funding for the service from the finance department, not to mention the fact that they need to get their team onboard using your new products.

They probably need to change internal procedures as a result of adopting your solution. It is a lot of work and change on their end. They need to have a very good reason to do so. The fact that your product has blue buttons and nice screens will not be a good enough reason. If your product can solve a problem that keeps them up at night, now *that* is a good reason – and they will act on it as a result.

Once you have done a few consultations and product demonstrations, you will discover that although your leads come from different companies, they face similar challenges. After awhile, you will be able to identify these challenges, and you should create solutions for them using your product. You should script it and have your sales team use these scripts when they identify these issues with their prospects.

The Takeaway

As you can see, *The Corporate Sales Formula* is very specific, tried, true and simple to follow. Notice I didn't say "easy". After all, if selling was easy, everyone would do it! Instead, I have tried to create a proven formula that not only works well most of the time, but is easy to use for new and experienced sales people alike.